WISDOM TREE

Contents

1. **Humility**   3

    Humility is not thinking less of yourself, it is thinking of yourself less.

2. **Develop Critical and Creative Thinking**   12

    We cannot solve our problems with the same thinking we used to create them.

3. **Developing Aesthetic Sense**   23

    Everything has its beauty but not everyone sees it.

4. **Doing the Right Thing**   32

    Knowing what is right doesn't mean much until you do what is right.

    How Can I Be More Involved?   40

5. **Dealing with Pressure**   42

    A diamond is a chunk of coal that did well under pressure.

6. **Learn to Question**   51

    "He who asks a question is a fool for five minutes; he who does not ask a question remains a fool forever."

7. **Human Rights**   61

    Give to every human being every right you claim for yourself.

    My Paragons   71

Humility

What is humility?

Humility is the quality of having a modest view of one's own importance. It is the ability to not accord too much importance to one's own self and abilities but to place them in context with that of others. It is the ability to understand the emotions of others and consider their happiness or sadness as important as our own.

Let us read the following extracts from the lives of some great men to know more about humility.

Our world has seen many a great men and women. Most of them have been blessed with the distinguished quality of humility. It is their humility among other things, that separates them from others. Also, this same humility makes them dear to those who know them. The following extract gives us a glimpse into their humility.

I. Theodore Roosevelt, the 26th President of the United States of America was once taking a walk at night along with his friend William Beebe. After looking at the sky for a while, Roosevelt pointed out a part of the night sky and said, "That is the Spiral Galaxy in the Andromeda. It is as large as our Milky Way. It is one of a hundred million galaxies. It consists of one hundred billion suns, each larger than our sun." Having recited all this, he added, "Now I think we are small enough! Let's go to bed."

II. It is said that Sir Winston Churchill, a former Prime Minister of the United Kingdom, was once asked if it thrilled him to know that every time he made a speech, the hall was always filled and there were many more who wished they had space to be in the hall to hear the speech. Sir Churchill in all his humility answered, "It's quite flattering but whenever I feel that way, I always remember that if instead of making a political speech I was being hanged, the crowd would be twice as big."

III. A scientist named George Washington Carver is famous for having developed over a hundred useful products from the peanut. These included cosmetics, dyes, paints, plastics and gasoline. He had also come up with around 105 recipes including the peanut. His research was centered on developing alternative crops to cotton, which provided food and nutrition to the people tilling the land in the USA. He once narrated a conversation between him and God.

George: "God, please tell me the mystery of the universe."

God: "I will not tell you that. The mystery of the universe is for me alone to know."

George: "God, then please tell me the mystery of the peanut."

God: "Now that, George, is more nearly your size. I am going to tell you the mystery of the peanut."

This is how he came to know so much about the peanut says George Washington Carver.

IV. Sir Walter Scott, the famous Scottish novelist, playwright and poet, was the leading literary figure in the whole of the United Kingdom. His position as the best literary figure alive was undisputed. While this was so, another person's writings started to gain popularity. This person was Lord Byron.

An anonymous critic praised Lord Byron's poems in a London paper. The critic said that the brilliance of the poetic genius was such that Scott could no longer be considered the leading poet of the United Kingdom. It was later discovered that the anonymous critic was none other than Sir Walter Scott himself!

V. A few soldiers were trying to move a heavy log off a road. A man mounted on a horse came by and saw that none could move on the road without the log being removed.

Sadly, the log was heavy and the men trying to heave it off were not able to do even with their combined effort.

The man who came by asked their commanding officer why he wasn't helping his men. The commanding officer barked, "I am the corporal. I give orders. It is my men's duty to work."

The man on the horse didn't like what he heard. He got off

his horse and helped the men to move the log. Together, they finally managed to remove the log. The path was now clear. The man came back to his horse. He mounted it and as he was about to journey ahead on the path, he said to the corporal, "Next time you need help, send for the commander-in-chief."

This man on the horse was none other than George Washington, the commander-in-chief and later the President of the United States of America.

Comprehension questions

Answer the following questions to test your understanding of the story.

1. "Now I think we are small enough! Let's go to bed." What do these line tell us about President Theodore Roosevelt?

   _____
   _____
   _____

2. Why does Sir Winston Churchill feel that there would be twice the size of crowd to see him hang, if he ever were to?

   _____
   _____
   _____

3. Why did God not give George Washington Carver the secret to the universe? Why did he reveal to him only the secret of the peanut?

   _____
   _____
   _____

4. It takes great humility to attribute greatness to another person, when you yourself have been acclaimed as the best. Which person in the above extract shows such humility?

   _____
   _____
   _____

5. What was the difference between the commander-in-chief and the corporal in the last extract above?
   _____
   _____
   _____

More about the Value

Humility is not undermining oneself. It is not demeaning oneself. It is accepting yourself and at the same time understanding that others are also important. Their emotions should also be taken into account.

As the British poet and novelist CS Lewis said,

> Humility is not thinking less of yourself, it is thinking of yourself less.
> — C S Lewis

Humble people are able to see themselves and others in perspective. They have a grasp over the true picture of the world around them.

Humility is a quality that will keep people in their place. It will help people avoid arrogance. They are never too full of themselves. Humble people are aware of what is happening around them. They listen to other people and understand their perspective.

Humility helps people see their own faults. This in turn helps people to better themselves. It allows us to appreciate the strengths of others and accept our own weaknesses. It allows us to be compassionate as we will be in a position to understand others emotions, both happiness and sadness. Humility allows us to progress and be peaceful.

> The humble man makes room for progress; the proud man believes he is already there.

A VALUE FOR ME
Humility is not thinking less of yourself, it is thinking of yourself less.

Snippet

Nelson Mandela, the famous South African anti-apartheid revolutionary and politician had to go underground for some time in the year 1961. His friend Wolfie Kodesh, a fellow activist, volunteered to hide Mandela in his home in Johannesburg.

The apartment was small and had just one bed and another folded camp cot. Kodesh offered the only bed to Mandela and he slept on the camp cot. He was trying to be a good host and showed respect to the famous revolutionary.

Kodesh revealed in his memoirs later that Mandela refused to take up the bed. He told Kodesh to sleep in his own bed because he was very tall unlike the shorter Mandela. Mandela slept on the camp cot during the eight weeks when he was at Kodesh's home.

Exercises

1. **Describe in five words what you think humility looks like in a person. Write another five words to describe what humility looks like in a society.**

Humility in a person	Humility in a society
1.	1.
2.	2.
3.	3.
4.	4.
5.	5.

2. **Cross out the words that you consider are not traits of a humble person.**

Arrogant	Dominating	Envious	Grateful
Modest	Plain	Proud	Self-righteous
Simple	Snobbish	Unassuming	Vain

3. Would you consider a person suffering from an inferiority complex or a person with humility? Why or why not? Discuss in 200 to 250 words.

   _____
   _____
   _____
   _____
   _____
   _____
   _____
   _____
   _____
   _____
   _____
   _____
   _____
   _____
   _____
   _____
   _____

4. Here are some rules in humility that are essential to any person and more so for a leader. Fill in the blanks to complete the sentences using appropriate words from the box.

   | Example | Publicity | Contribute | Listen | Know |

   a. Know what you don't _____.

   b. Avoid looking for your own _____.

   c. _____ to everyone because everyone has an idea.

   d. Pitch in. Everyone, even the leader has to _____ to the work of the team.

   e. Lead by _____ and not by mere words.

3. **Pick an article from a newspaper or a magazine that displays humility / vain in a person or an establishment. Explain your view on the article and share it with your classmates.**

_____
_____
_____
_____
_____
_____
_____
_____
_____
_____
_____
_____
_____
_____
_____

Test yourself

Take the following test to check your humility quotient.

1. Do you like to have your own picture with no one else in it, put up on the walls of your room?

    a. Yes	b. No

2. Imagine your grandmother is the President of India. You don't like others to treat you better or worse because you are the President's grandchild.

    a. Yes, you want to be treated as every other child is treated

    b. No, you expect to be treated specially because you the President's grandchild.

3. You help your friend rescue a cat from a tree. People praise you and not your friend. Do you

   a. let it pass

   b. correct them and tell them that your friend had done more to rescue the ca

4. When you win an international prize in mathematics,

   a. you do not want your parents to talk about it because you do not want to appear proud.

   b. you don't mind your parents talk about it because you have worked hard for it.

5. Do you ask

   a. what you can do for your country

   b. what your country can do for you

   If your answers are 1.b, 2.a, 3.b, 4.b and 5.a, you are a humble person.

Tips to Parents and Teachers

Humility comes with the ability to keep others before self. This does not mean one has to undermine oneself or sacrifice his or her own interests. This fine balance is difficult to achieve and yet important to raise kind, compassionate and humble children.

Develop self-esteem in children. Let them learn to appreciate their worth. However they also need to be able to recognize their limitations and drawbacks. They should be taught to appreciate others. They should be able to acknowledge others for their help. Another aspect of humble people is their ability to listen to others. Teach the child to wait for their turn to speak. Make them understand that it is as important to listen to others as it is to voice themselves.

> "Humility is the only true wisdom by which we prepare our minds for all the possible changes of life."
>
> — George Arliss

Do's and Don'ts

1. Learn to accept that while you may be good at things, there will be others who are better than you. This does not mean that you undermine yourself. It simply means that you know your place and compete in a healthy manner to improve yourself, if you wish to.

2. Introspection is essential. Learn to analyze your actions and see your own flaws. Understand that neither no one is perfect nor is anyone always right. You too could be at fault.

3. Recognize your positives and your blessings. Be grateful for what you have. While you may desire more, there are many in the world who do not have and are craving for what you have.

4. You may be a hardworking person and an achiever. Remember that your achievements are possible because of others and their help as well.

5. When you make a mistake, admit that you have done so. This doesn't make you a lesser person. It only makes you humble.

6. Be considerate while you speak. Take into account others while you speak. Ensure that you do not utter anything that could cause others discomfort or hurt them.

7. Avoid boasting.

> Humility is the ability to give up your pride and yet retain your dignity.

Develop Critical and Creative Thinking

What is critical thinking? How is it different from creative thinking?

Critical thinking is thinking and judging for one's self. It is the thinking to assess for ourselves, the existing ideas, notions and concepts so that we may not blindly follow them but understand them. Once we understand them, we are at liberty to follow or reject them because of our own conviction. Critical thinking helps in filtering out unwanted assumptions, superstitions and so on and helps us and our society to progress.

Creative thinking is the ability to think creatively. In other words, it is the ability to develop unique ideas.

It is essential to develop both critical and creative thinking. While one helps to judge for ourselves, the other helps to create new things. They are both essential for progress.

Let us read the following story to understand more about critical thinking.

Have you heard of the hare who thought the sky was falling? Well, there lived a hare in a forest, many years ago. While enjoying a siesta under a tree one hot afternoon something fell on its head. The hare woke up with a start.

Perhaps it was the heat that played tricks with its head or perhaps it was a dream that it thought true or perhaps it was indeed true, but the hare thought that the sky was falling. "No one was safe! They will all die if the sky did fall on them," thought the hare.

It shot up from its comfortable place under the tree and ran as fast as it could. On the way, it met a deer, chomping on the soft green grass. The deer said, "Why in such a hurry dear hare? Surely you are not running another race!"

The hare did not bother to stop. It however replied even while on the run, "The sky is falling! Run if you want to live."

The deer naturally panicked. It definitely did not want to die with the sky falling on its head. And so it dashed as fast as it could behind the hare. A few other animals saw the deer and the hare streak past them.

"Run for your lives! The sky is falling!" shouted the hare and the deer in tandem. The other animals did not need telling twice. With every wish to stay alive, they too scampered and hastened as best as they could behind the two that streaked by.

As you can guess by now, soon almost all the animals in the forest were hurrying out of it to escape the falling sky.

It was only at long last and at the behest of the terrifying lion that all the animals halted. Though fearing the falling sky, their fear of the lion was also such that they had to put a break to their attempt to get away as fast as they could.

"I demand to know which of you saw the sky falling," roared the lion. A trembling hare came forward and informed that it was he who saw the sky falling.

"Lead me to that place. I want to see for myself for I do not think the sky can indeed fall on us," said the lion. Much as it was scared of returning to the place where the sky had begun to fall, the hare could not dare to disobey a direct command from the king of the jungle.

So it led the lion to where it had taken a nap earlier that afternoon.

Surprisingly, the sky was still up in the sky where it belonged to. The lion smirked at the hare and began looking around. Then the hare found that it was an acorn that had fallen on its head. The acorn caused the hare to awake from a deep sleep and it mistook the acorn for the sky falling!

> Read not to contradict and confute; nor to believe and take for granted; nor to find talk and discourse; but to weigh and consider.
>
> — Sir Francis Bacon

Having understood about critical thinking, let us now read another story to understand about creative thinking.

Chester Greenwood was a thirteen-year-old boy living in 1873. He was perhaps just like any other boy his age and could not resist the temptation of ice-skating on a cold December day. Now anyone who has experienced sub zero temperatures would know how chillingly cold it could be to play outdoors in snow and how important it is to keep one's ears covered. Chester was desperate to play, but, at the same time he had to protect himself from the cold. He found a piece of wire and with his grandmother's help, he padded the ends of the wire. He then clipped this wire to his head, the padded portions covering his ears. He was safe from the cold and could play to his heart's content on the ice.

In the beginning, he was ridiculed by his friends for wearing such a contraption over his ears. However, soon they realized that while they had to head indoors to keep themselves from freezing, Chester was able to play and skate for longer because of his ear coverings. They began asking Chester to make some more ear coverings for them too.

That was the beginning of the modern day earmuffs.

> We cannot solve our problems with the same thinking we used to create them.
>
> — Albert Einstein

Comprehension questions

Answer the following questions to test your understanding of the narrations.

1. Why did the hare run for its life?

　_____
　_____
　_____

2. Do you agree that most animals of the forest showed mob mentality? How can you gather from the story of the hare that mob mentality is generally bereft of critical thinking?

　_____
　_____
　_____

3. What do you understand by critical thinking from this story? Why do you think it is important to think critically?

　_____
　_____
　_____

4. Why was Chester able to play for a longer time in the cold than the other children around him?

　_____
　_____
　_____

5. What do you gather from creative thinking from the story of Chester Greenwood?

　_____
　_____
　_____

More about the Value

Critical and creative thinking takes training. You need to exercise your mind and train it to be able to think critically as well as creatively. The following pointers will help you think critically:

- You should be able to identify assumptions and generalizations around you – both what people carry and what you yourself have. When you are able to identify the assumptions, you will be able to analyze and judge for yourself.
- Learn to question the validity of any information whether it is existing knowledge or new ideas that you come across. Do not take any information for granted. Look deeper and see for yourself if there is any truth to it.
- Be true to yourself when you judge or analyze information. For instance, you may come across a claim on a social website. Do not accept it without checking the information for its validity.
- Look for logic in your thought and actions.
- Look for the source of any information you receive. Learn to judge the source. Do not trust blindly in anything.

Critical thinking is a skill that you will need more and more as you grow up. In future academic researches, you will need to look at the plethora of available information critically. You will need critical thinking to separate the chaff. You will need to do the same to filter out unwanted, redundant and detrimental information to ensure that your work is progressive.

> Education is not the learning of facts but the training of the mind to think.
> — Albert Einstein

Likewise, creative thinking is essential to be able to come up with new solutions and ideas. Here are some pointers that will help you to be a creative thinker:

- Learn to question things. When you question the validity of things, you will be able to think for yourself and think differently.
- Never stop the process of learning. Never think that you know everything or you know enough.
- Set yourself goals. Aim to achieve them.
- Don't be afraid of trying out new things.
- Come up with many solutions to one problem or rather many ways to solving a problem.

> An essential aspect of creativity is not being afraid to fail.
> — Edwin Land

A VALUE FOR ME

We cannot solve our problems with the same thinking we used to create them.

Snippet

Mrs. Earl Dickson was what one would call an inexperienced cook. She was perhaps callous or plainly unlucky for she often injured herself through a burn or a cut while working in her kitchen.

Her husband, Mr. Dickson, was an employee of the Johnson and Johnson, a medical devices and pharmaceutical company. With an intention to helping his wife, he began preparing bandages in advance so that his wife could apply them herself even when he wasn't at home if she hurts herself.

This was how the world's first adhesive strip bandages came into existence.

These stories teach us that critical and creative thinking are essential for progress and to find solutions to simple and complex problems.

Exercises

. **Here is an exercise to put your critical thinking to test. Following are some sentences. Tick those that are factual and those that are opinions.**

a. A cow is the most useful animal on earth. ☐

b. My mother is the best mother. ☐

c. The sun is one of the millions of stars in our galaxy. ☐

d. Telephone numbers are difficult to remember. ☐

e. The tallest mountain on land is the Mount Everest. ☐

f. Smoking is injurious to health. ☐

g. Humans blink to protect their eyes. ☐

h. Santa Claus doesn't exist. ☐

2. The following is a famous painting by Edvard Munch. He created four versions of the same painting between 1893 and 1910. Such is the fame of this painting that it had been subjected to several attempts of theft from various museums.

After looking at the picture, give your own interpretation of the painting. Why do you think the person or thing in the painting has the expression shown? Write your views in 50 to 100 words. Compare your views with those of your friends. You may be surprised to see the different thoughts each of you has come up with. Later, search the internet to find the inspiration behind the painting by Munch. You may be even more surprised by it.

_____
_____
_____
_____
_____
_____
_____

This exercise shows you the power of creative thinking. It provides several perspectives to one event. It helps you to develop tolerance.

3. Pick any advertisement of your choice. Collect a cutout from the newspaper of any other source of your choice. Paste it in the space below. Now analyze the advertisement and critically review its truthfulness and its impact.

4. **Pick a standard board of the game snakes and ladders. Usually, most of these boards have ladders and snakes on a grid of 10 X 10. When the player gets to a ladder, he or she is given a leg up to a higher box and when the player comes across a snake, he or she is sent back in the race.**

   Make it a fun activity. Give reasons for getting a leg up or being brought down. Your reasons should revolve around the various values you have learnt so far. Display of a good value should be the incentive for a ladder and display of any vice should be the reason for a snake sending you down.

   You could draw your own game on a chart paper.

5. What would happen if human beings lose the ability to speak on a particular day of the week. For instance, no person can speak on a Thursday. Write a short essay on the consequences of such a happening.

   _____
   _____
   _____
   _____
   _____
   _____
   _____
   _____

Test yourself

Take the following test to check if you can think critically and creatively.

1. Do you consider the pros and cons of any action that you undertake?

    a. Yes				b. No

2. Do you accept things handed down to you through the generations without questioning them?

    a. Yes				b. No

3. When faced with a problem, do you wait for someone to offer you a solution?

    a. Yes				b. No				c. Not always

4. Do you enjoy painting, drawing or creating music?

    a. Yes				b. No

5. Do you look for ways in which you could simplify your work?

    a. Yes				b. No

*If your answers are 1.a, 2.b, 3.b or c, 4.a and 5.a, then your brain is thinking both critically and creatively.

Tips to Parents and Teachers

Children should be able to see themselves as problem solvers. They should be able to think of every situation for themselves, see its good and bad, think about its pros and cons and arrive at a decision on how to react. They should be able to come up with solutions creatively as well as critically.

For this, encourage children to think about situations around them. Never snub them when they come up with questions. Help them probe for answers and solutions. Spoon-feeding is not acceptable, especially at this age when they start to behave as young adults.

Children may not be able to solve all their problems by themselves. You may need to intervene or help them by guiding them in the right path. However, let them think for themselves first. Let them stumble a bit before you offer them help.

Encourage out of the box thinking.

Dos and Don'ts

1. Never judge a situation immediately. Be open-minded. Analyze the situation and defer judgment for a later time. Instead, look at the possibilities.
2. Learn to look at a situation or a problem from different perspectives.
3. Learn to think logically. The result is always a possibility of working in a sequential and organized manner.
4. You may come up with a new or a creative idea by sometimes doing things out of the routine. A change in habit may bring about a change in thought too.
5. Learn to communicate with people.
6. Listening to others is very important to both creative and critical thinking.
7. Learn to question and seek answers.
8. Never assume that you know everything. Your humility will help you think creatively.

Developing Aesthetic Sense

What is aesthetics?
Aesthetics comes from a Greek word 'aistehesis' which means recognition via the senses. Aesthetics is a branch of philosophy. It deals with understanding the nature of art, beauty and taste. It also deals with the creation and appreciation of beauty.

Let us read the following piece of writing about Aesthetics to understand more about it.

Everywhere we look around, we see things that have been built with care and accuracy. From the phone you speak into every day to the books you read day and night and even the pen that you hold every time you need to write down something for a school assignment, things have come into existence after a considerable amount of thought, experimentation, rejection and acceptance of the idea, the concept and the design.

We may take for granted the convenience of a small handheld lightweight phone or a sleek pen that runs along smoothly on a paper. However, many brains would have gone into designing them to suit our liking.

Aesthetics is involved in all of this process. Every piece that we use is made in such a way that it appeals to our taste and in addition suit our convenience. Ease of use is also taken into account while building these.

One of the most sought after product in the world today is perhaps an Apple device. Be it the iPhone, the iPad or the mac computers, their aesthetic designs have captured the hearts of many world over. The simplicity of design both inside and out is what adds to its beauty according to tech critics. The founder of Apple products, Steve Jobs, has attributed his aesthetic sense to Zen Buddhism and the simplicity in it among other things.

Aesthetic sense is culture specific. Some cultures promote subtle and light colours while others recommend bold hues; some cultures look at simplicity while others aim for grandiosity. However, despite differences and varying types of art manifestations, human beings are universally capable of appreciating art and things of beauty.

While Zen Buddhism may have influenced the design of the current Apple products, the Gothic architecture of the high and late medieval period of Europe was influenced by the political and religious atmosphere prevalent in Europe at that time. The flourishing trade during relatively peaceful times during the medieval era allowed for huge funds. The presence of the Catholic Church in mainland Europe was also responsible for the majestic and intricately designed Gothic structures of that era, some of which stand in their glory even to this day.

All in all, it is beneficial to be able to take time out to appreciate things made well because it gives us satisfaction. It helps us to build and design things which are more useful and easy to use.

Comprehension questions

Answer the following questions to test your understanding of aesthetic sense.

1. Mention some of the aspects stated in the essay above that go into designing any product.

   _____
   _____
   _____

2. How do aesthetics and ease of use go hand in hand?

   _____
   _____
   _____

3. Which religious philosophy inspired the design sensibilities of Apple?

   _____
   _____
   _____

4. What were the leading factors that led to the development of Gothic structures in medieval Europe?

   _____
   _____
   _____

5. Why is it beneficial to develop a sense of aesthetics?

_____
_____
_____

More about the Value

Aesthetics governs many aspects of our lives. Cultures evolve around their idea of aesthetics. Monuments, pieces of art, poetry, prose etc. are built around aesthetics. Aesthetics is not limited to only such artistic things. Even buildings of everyday use, the layout of rooms, the arrangement of furniture in a room or books on a bookshelf; and the things that are used everyday involve aesthetics.

> Everything has its beauty but not everyone sees it.
> — Confucius

It is important to be able to create things with an aesthetic sense because it helps us develop a sense of proportion, harmony and beauty. An aesthetically designed app will help the user to feel comfortable and use it well. It will help the user remain in a calm and content mood and will thereby help him or her work better. Likewise, working in an aesthetically built building helps to calm the mind and give an elevated feeling. It lends to better work performance. It also helps in our emotional development.

> Rules of taste enforce the structures of power.
> — Susan Sontag

A VALUE FOR ME
Everything has its beauty but not everyone sees it.

Snippet

On an ordinary morning in January, 2007, a man started playing the violin at a metro station in Washington DC. People in the metro station were in a hurry and hardly took notice of this man. Three minutes after he started playing the instrument, he had his first audience. An elderly man slowed down, listened to him for a few seconds and went ahead on his way. A few minutes later, another man stopped to listen to him, gave him a coin, and went on. Some more minutes passed by and a young boy of around three years of age wanted to stay and listen, but the boy's mother tugged him along. While he walked away holding his mother's hand, he kept turning around to observe the violinist. This trend continued for the entire forty five minutes that the man played. Very few stopped to listen to him. Those who stopped, did so only for a few seconds. Most of them who wanted to stop were children, but their parents hurried them along. Even fewer of those who paused to listen offered money.

1097 people passed by the musician in those forty-five minutes. Only seven stopped to listen for a short while. Twenty people paused to drop in some money before continuing on their way. His total collection was 32 dollars and 17 cents.

When he finished playing, he simply picked up his instrument and walked away. No one noticed him leave. There was no applause of any kind.

Now, one may ask what was so special about this violinist? Unknown to the people at the metro station, the man was playing some of the most intricate pieces of music ever written. He was playing on a violin worth 3.5 million dollars. He was Joshua Bell, a highly acclaimed and accomplished musician.

A couple of days prior to this incident, people had paid 100 dollars each to listen to the same musician at a theater in Boston, where he played the same music.

This was an experiment conducted by the Washington Post to know more about perception, taste and people's priorities. Not many noticed the musician playing at the metro station either because they were in a hurry or because they did not expect a piece of beauty at such a place. This episode should teach us that beauty is all around us; we may be missing it in the rushed lives we lead or because we do not look for it everywhere.

Exercises

1. Aesthetics is about appreciating beauty. You could begin by looking at yourself. Learn to appreciate what you are. Describe yourself in a not less than 12 adjectives.

   _____ _____ _____ _____
   _____ _____ _____ _____
   _____ _____ _____ _____
   _____ _____ _____ _____

2. The following are few rhyming words. Create a poem using these rhyming words.

Plate	eight	Humming	coming
Greenery	Scenery	Mightily	Vitally
Blue	Shoe	Plop	Shop
Smile	Mile	Tall	Wall

27

3. **Say true or false.**

   a. Aesthetics is an appreciation for art and beauty. ☐

   b. Aesthetics involves the senses of only sight and smell. ☐

   c. All human beings including children and adults are capable of experiencing art. ☐

   d. Aesthetics appeal means 'I like and enjoy what I see.' ☐

   e. Aesthetics governs only the way we see and enjoy things around us. It influences us in no other way. ☐

   f. The capacity for aesthetics is a characteristic of all human beings. ☐

4. **Select any monument, gadget or advertisement of your choice. Paste a picture or sketch it out in the space below. Describe in about 250 words how the monument appeals to you aesthetically.**

5. Aesthetics evoke not merely a sense of satisfaction or joy in us but also affect the way we respond to situations. A well designed building helps us function better. A well designed advertisement serves its purpose by ingraining itself in people's memory. A well designed gadget apart from looking wonderful is easy to use.

Considering these factors, would you consider your school building aesthetically built or would you want it to be built differently? Put on your thinking hats and recommend changes to the design of your school to have a more aesthetic appeal. If you think your school is well designed, critically appreciate the design.

You could express your views in words or in pictorial form.

Test yourself

Answer the following to test your ability to appreciate art and beauty.

1. I like to read fiction.

   a. Yes   b. No

2. I like to create things.

   a. Yes   b. No

3. I can appreciate the beauty in words as well as the beauty in numbers

   a. Yes   b. No

4. I may not sing but I definitely enjoy music.

   a. Yes   b. No

5. Technology interests me, not paintings, dance and music.

   a. Yes   b. No

*Whatever your answers to the above are, as long as you are able to appreciate the beauty of anything, be it books, paintings, music, dance, technology or even the goodness in people, you have an aesthetic sense. Everyone is born with it. We merely need to acknowledge and develop it because it has its benefits.

Tips to Parents and Teachers

Help children to see the world through all their senses. Let them taste, smell, hear and see things as well as feel things. Encourage them to be more aware of their surroundings. Teach them to observe the good in people and things around them. When they are able to appreciate the beauty of things, they will be able to enjoy their lives even in the humdrum of things. They will be able to find peace and solace through such things. This will in turn help them to live a stress free life. It will help them to be peaceful people.

Dos and Don'ts

1. Take time out to look at things and enjoy them. There are lots of things around you that would instill a sense of joy because of their beauty and aesthetics.
2. When you like what someone has done, be it a sketch or a melodious rendition, be sure to appreciate the artist.
3. Look for beauty in yourself and others. Kindness, generosity, humility and affection are some qualities that lend to beauty in a person.
4. Appreciate simplicity.
5. Learn to reject what is not appealing.
6. It takes time to develop an aesthetic sense.

> Beauty lies in the eyes of the beholder.

Doing the Right Thing

What is 'right thing'? Why should we do the right thing?
Things that are correct and are in accordance with an acceptable value system are called right things. All the values that we learn are an attempt to ensure that we learn what the right thing to do is. Knowing right from wrong is one thing but doing the right thing however difficult it might be or however tempting the wrong thing might be is important. Our actions define us and doing the right thing automatically ensures that we turn out to be good people.

Let us read the following story to understand more about Doing the Right Thing.

Let us look at the world of sports to understand more about doing the right thing. Read the following true incident to appreciate the importance of doing the right thing even under pressure in a highly competitive field such as sports.

Spain was hosting a cross-country race in December 2012. Among the several participants were Olympic bronze medalist Abel Mutai and another promising athlete Ivan Fernandez Anaya. The Olympic champion was in the lead position while the young athlete Ivan was second in the race. With only a few meters to go to the finish line, Abel Mutai stopped running. He was falsely under the impression that he had crossed the finish line. The younger runner Ivan soon caught up with Abel. He knew the finish line was still a distance away. Instead of running ahead to claim victory, he informed Abel of his mistake and coaxed him to start running to the actual finish line. Ivan let Abel finish first, and claim victory for the race.

Though people say all is fair in love and war, Ivan did not consider running ahead to the finish line in this scenario correct. He knew his victory would then be only because of somebody else's mistake and not because of his own ability. That notion did not sit well with his conscience.

Commenting on the incident, Ivan Fernandez Anaya later said,

"I didn't deserve to win. I did what I had to do. He was the rightful winner."

Comprehension questions

Answer the following questions to test your understanding of positivity.

1. Who was the Olympic medalist who was the clear champion for most of the cross-country race held in Spain?

   _____
   _____
   _____

2. Who is the other athlete in the story? At what position was he in the race?

   _____
   _____
   _____

3. Why had the lead runner stopped before the finish line?

   _____
   _____
   _____

4. What did Ivan do when he realized the lead athlete's folly?

   _____
   _____
   _____

5. What would you have done had you been in Ivan's position?

   _____
   _____
   _____

6. What would you have done had you been in Abel's position?

   _____
   _____
   _____

More about the Value

> It's the action not the fruit of the action that's important. You have to do the right thing. It may not be in your power, may not be in your time that there will be any fruit. But that doesn't mean you stop doing the right thing. You may never know what results come from your action. But if you do nothing, there will be no result.
> — Mahatma Gandhi

There was once a person working as a manager for an extremely rich man. The manager was swindling the rich man, though by meager portions, for his own benefit. Soon the rich man discovered that the manager was cheating him of his money, so he fired him.

Jesus told the above story to his disciples and then explained that when a person cannot be trusted with little, the person cannot be trusted with much. Likewise, he added that a person who is dishonest even in the slightest is capable of being dishonest in large measures too. Therefore, it is essential to do the right thing always so that one's integrity and respect are never lost.

> The right thing to do and the hard thing to do are usually the same.
> — Steve Maroboli

A VALUE FOR ME

Knowing what is right doesn't mean much until you do what is right.

Snippet

Read the following Aesop's fable to know of another aspect of doing the right thing.

A fisherman, who also happened to be a skilled flautist, once took his fishing nets as well as his flute to the sea. He laid his nets in the shallow water and started playing his flute. He thought that the fish would get mesmerized by his music and on their own accord get into his fishing nets. But to his surprise, this did not happen. He played his flute to his heart's content till he was out of breath, but not a single fish was caught in his nets.

Finally, he laid aside his flute and cast his nets into deeper water. He returned with a good catch. Can you guess what he said to the fish as they jumped about in his nets trying to catch a breath of life?

He said, "You wretched creatures! When I piped the most melodious of tunes, you did not dance. Now that I have stopped playing, you leap and bounce about so energetically!"

> Doing the right thing at the right time is an art.

Exercises

1. Is anything wrong with the line 'finders keepers, losers weepers'. Express your views through a poster.

2. Was there ever anything that you wanted to do desperately knowing well that it wasn't the right thing to do? Did you succumb to your temptation and do it or did you stand by what you considered right and not do it?

    Mention how you handled the situation and what you felt through the entire experience.

    _____
    _____
    _____
    _____
    _____
    _____
    _____
    _____
    _____
    _____
    _____
    _____
    _____
    _____
    _____

3. Is there ever a right time to do the wrong thing? Is it ever okay to do the wrong thing? Search through stories you know if you can justify this. Mention the story that you picked in the box below. Discuss your reasons in class and convince your friends of your stand point.

4. **Solve the crossword with the help of the clues below.**

1. People who tend to do the right things will lose _____ friends and gain true friends.

2. Doing the right thing means _____ between the right and the wrong.

3. _____ need to always choose the right thing to do over the wrong, because their actions affect the entire team.

4. Picking the wrong thing to do may be _____ but in the long run is never good for anyone.

5. Doing the right thing never really harms _____.

6. _____ right from wrong is not enough. You need to be able to do the right thing.

7. You need _____ to do the right thing.

5. Keep a journal for a week. Note down instances where you had to decide between what is right and wrong. Also mention the reason that led you to make your choice between the right and the wrong thing to do.

Sl. No.	When I had to choose between doing the right and wrong thing	What I chose	The reason why I chose it
1.			
2.			
3.			
4.			
5.			
6.			
7.			
8.			

Test yourself

Answer the following to test your ability to appreciate art and beauty.

1. Do you consider your conscience while making a decision?

   a. Yes   b. No

2. Do you believe in doing something even if it hurts others?

   a. Yes   b. No

3. Have you ever apologized to someone because you had done the wrong thing?

   a. Yes   b. No

4. Do you have the willpower to do something right even though it is tough?

   a. Yes   b. No

5. Do you feel bad inside when you don't do the right thing?

   a. Yes   b. No

*If your answers are 1.a, 2.b, 3.a, 4.a and 5.a, then you are on the right path. You believe in doing the right thing and have been successful in doing it too.

Tips to Parents and Teachers

Right actions come from right thoughts. At an age where children start showing a lesser dependence on their parents or teachers for their decisions, it is essential that they are capable of thinking right. Encourage good thoughts. Voice yourself about issues and let them understand or know your views on things. Children learn through emulation. If they see you do the right thing and live with integrity, they too will be motivated to stick by their morals.

Doing the right thing may not always be easy. People may not stand with them because of their actions. It is times like these that parents and teachers need to stick by them and reinforce the belief that they need to do the right thing no matter what the sacrifice is.

Never shun their decisions out rightly. Understand why they think so and act so before guiding them onto the right path. Help them learn to foresee the outcome of their actions. Teach them empathy. Let them be responsible for their actions whether good or bad. When they are able to accept responsibility for their actions, they will be more cautious about their deeds. They will think before acting and therefore will be encouraged to do the right thing.

Do's and Don'ts

1. Listen to your inner voice. Your conscience is your best guide.
2. Never do anything that hurts others. However, if your actions are right and it hurts a person who is in the wrong, do not hesitate from doing what is right even if it hurts the other person.
3. Fairness is not always a people pleaser. You may be in the danger of losing friends or popularity while doing the right thing. However, you will win true friends in the long run when you do what is right.
4. Think of the consequences before doing anything.
5. Think of the adults you respect before doing something. Consider how your actions will be viewed by them.
6. If you are ever in doubt about what you should do, never hesitate to ask your elders to guide you on the right path.

How Can I Be More Involved?

When you look at the world around you, don't you feel a sense of belonging and responsibility? Collect pictures of your concerns from your surroundings, from newspapers and magazines. Paste them here and write how you feel about them and what you insist on doing about them.

Dealing with Pressure

What is pressure? Why is dealing with pressure important?
Pressure is an attempt by external factors to force someone or influence someone to behave or act in certain ways. When there is a lot to be done and very little time, resource or talent to accomplish it, one finds himself or herself under pressure. Pressure is stressful. It often leads people to act against their better judgment. Being under pressure is never good for health. It is important to overcome the feelings that we get when we are under pressure to ensure good health and a good result.

Let us read the following story to understand more about dealing with pressure.

A philosophy professor once walked into his class with an empty glass jar. He placed the jar on a desk. He then took out some golf balls from his bag. The students in the class were now watching him with interest. The professor then dropped the golf balls into the jar until they had reached the brim. There was no space left in the jar for even one more golf ball.

Once this was done, the professor faced his students and asked them, "Is this glass jar full now?"

The unanimous response from the students was, "Yes."

The professor then dug out another box from his bag. This box was full of pebbles. He poured the pebbles into the glass jar. Surprisingly, the pebbles rolled into the spaces between the golf balls. Quite a lot of pebbles could be accommodated in the glass jar.

He once again asked his students if they thought that the jar was full.

This time, the class was not spontaneous or confident of their answer. Some answered with a 'yes' while others were skeptical. They did not answer.

The professor then took out another box from his bag. This box contained sand.

He started pouring the sand into the glass jar, which was already filled to the brim with golf balls and pebbles. Surprisingly, the sand simply sifted into the glass jar and settled well in the spaces between the pebbles and the golf balls.

"Now do you think that the glass jar is full?" asked the professor.

Most students said 'yes.' After all what else could fit in the jar which had the empty spaces filled with sand?

The professor then put his hand into his bag. The class became curious to see what else he would pull out of the bag.

This time, the professor pulled out a bottle of water. He poured the water into the jar. The jar had some space left in it to accommodate a bit of water as well.

The students were both amused and stunned. The professor then explained that each of the students needs to remember that the jar was their life. When you consider your life is full of activity and you are left with no time for anything else, be it friends, family, sports or other passions, one should remember the jar that could accommodate golf balls, pebbles, sand and water. There is always space for things.

Also, another way of looking at the jar and its contents is to consider the golf balls as friends and family. They are the most important things in one's life. The pebbles represent things like one's job, house, car, etc. They are important, yet minor concerns in life. The sand and the water are other minor things in life. If you fill up your life first with minor things like sand and water, there will not be any place for the most important things that are represented by the golf balls. It is important to prioritize life so that one may live and enjoy it to its fullest.

These two attitudes are important to be able to deal with pressure.

Comprehension questions

Answer the following questions to check your understanding of the story.

1. What were the various things that the professor put into the glass jar?
   _____
   _____
   _____

2. Why do you think each time the professor could keep filling up the jar even when there seemed to be no place left in it?
   _____
   _____
   _____

3. Do you think it would be possible for the professor to put in the things if he changed the order in which he put them in?
   _____
   _____
   _____

4. What are the various things that the professor compares the golf balls, the pebbles, the sand and the water to?
   _____
   _____
   _____

5. Summarize in two or three lines the lesson on dealing with pressure that the professor tries to teach his students through the experiment he conducts in class.
   _____
   _____
   _____

More about the Value

As they say, pressure creates diamond. However, it is essential to develop the strength to deal with pressure. Modern lifestyles, pace and demands have put a lot of people, both children and adults under pressure. There is pressure to compete and win; pressure to stand up to the expectations of parents, teachers and others and the pressure to be accepted by peers. It is easy to give into pressure and act rashly or get into depression. Therefore, it is essential to learn to deal with pressure and come out successfully rather than buckle and ruin yourself or your chances at happiness or success.

Let us look at some ways in which one can handle pressure. First and foremost, accept that you are not the only one going through difficult times. Be humble enough to accept that yours are not the only troubles in the world. There are people around you who are going through their own troubles. Each of these are big enough and you can help yourself and others around you with a positive attitude.

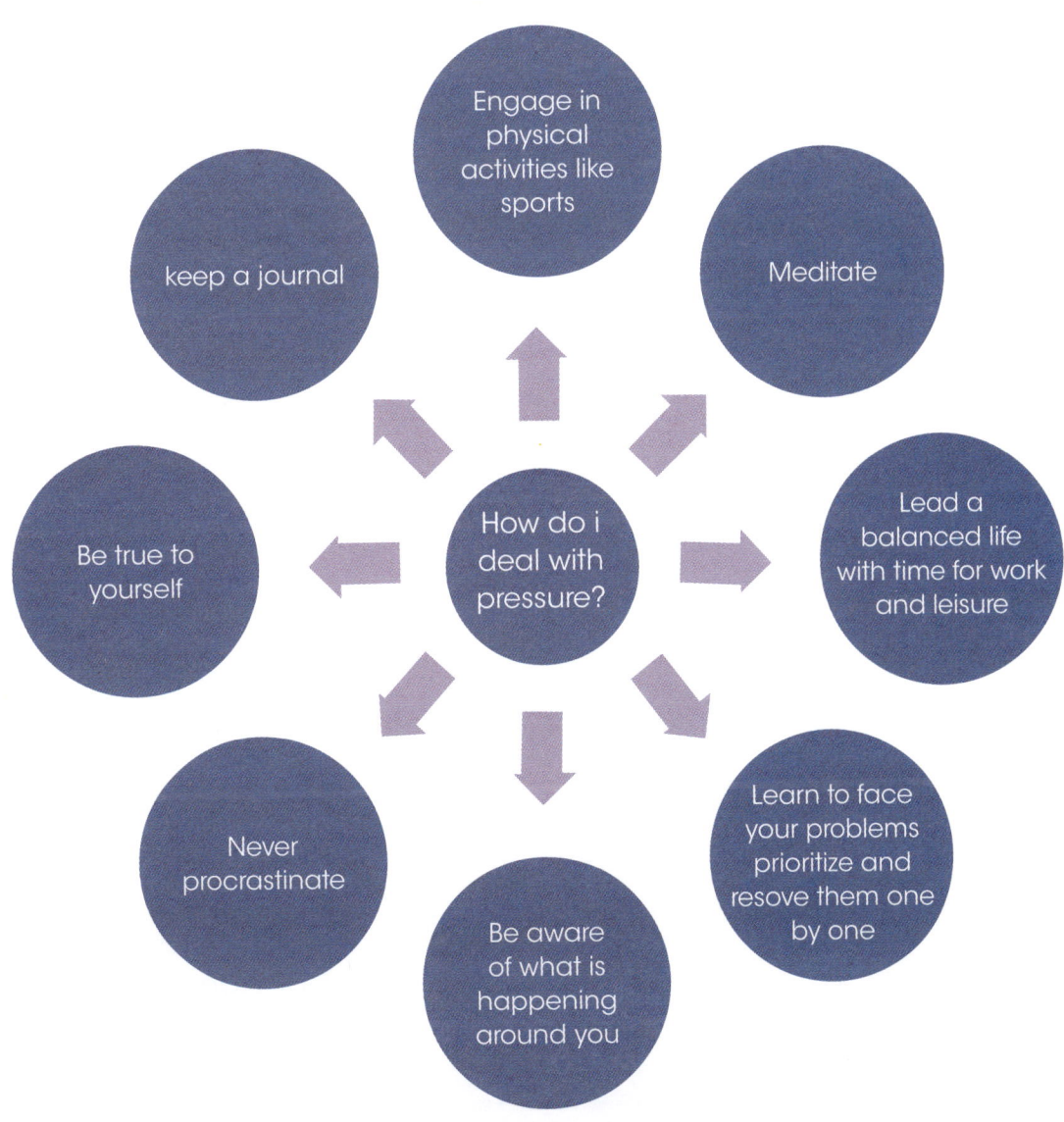

A VALUE FOR ME
*A diamond
is a chunk of coal that did well under pressure.*

Snippet

One cold winter evening, just as it began to snow, a man named Sam noticed that his colleague was having trouble with his car. He did not know the man well but knew that he too worked in the same office as he did. Sam offered to help the other. Since all the car workshops were closed down for the evening, they decided to leave the broken down car in the office parking lot and get it checked the next day.

Sam offered to drop off the Phil (that was the second man's name) at his home that evening and pick him up for work the next day. They drove along in silence.

When they reached Phil's home, Phil got down, thanked Sam and walked up to his door. While pulling out of the driveway, Sam noticed Phil pause at a tree right outside his front door, touch it fondly with both hands before entering his warm home.

The next morning, while waiting in the car for his colleague, Sam noticed that Phil once again touched the tree while coming out of his home.

Intrigued by this action, Sam asked Phil why he touched the tree while going into and coming out of his home.

Phil said, "That is my worry tree. I pass on my day's worries from work to the tree. When I do this, I am able to greet my wife and children with a smile. I am able to enjoy the evening in their company. The next morning, when I head out to work, I pick up my worries from the tree. The surprising part is that, most of the time, there aren't as many worries to pick up as I had hung there the previous evening."

It is important to let go of worries in life. When we carry our worries we only amplify the worries. This stops us from enjoying life to its fullest.

Exercises

1. Identify the emotions you experience when you are under pressure. Circle your answers

abandoned	alone	angry
attractive	calm	confused
cool	curious	disrespected
embarrassed	excited	ignorant
important	in control	invisible
nervous	obvious	out of control
powerless	scared	smart
stupid	ugly	unimportant

2. One of the ways to avoid being under pressure and getting stressed is to be confident about yourself. Make a list of your accomplishments. This will help you boost up your ego and remain confident. Never doubt yourself.

My Accomplishments

_____
_____
_____
_____
_____
_____
_____
_____
_____
_____

3. Is there anything that you feel diffident about? What makes you feel pressured When do you succumb to pressure and stress? Make a list here and analyz if you need to feel the pressure. Also write ways in which you should handle these situations that make you feel the pressure.

Sl. No.	What puts me under pressure	How should I tackle this

4. Often teenagers fall prey to vices like drugs, smoking or drinking. This ma be because of peer pressure or a way to handle pressure and stress from elsewhere.

Make a poster, advising teenagers not to do drugs, or take up smoking an drinking.

5. **Choose the correct options from below to complete the sentences.**

   a. Learn to say _____. You needn't do things that put you under pressure.

      i. Yes   ii. No

   b. Stick to _____. Regular schedules lessen the burden on a person and thereby reduce the chances of feeling the pressure.

      i. a routine   ii. Chaos

   c. Being under pressure affects your _____.

      i. health   ii. wealth

   d. Peer group pressure is the pressure you feel because of the _____ that you belong to.

      i. country   ii. group of similar aged people

Test yourself

Take the following test to check if you are a determined person.

1. Do you sleep the required 8 hours every day at a stretch?

   a. Yes   b. No

2. Do you enjoy comfort foods like chocolates and chips when you are nervous?

   a. Yes   b. No

3. Do you have at least one person you can call a good friend on whom you can depend, no matter what?

   a. Yes   b. No

4. Do you exercise adequately, to the point of perspiration, every day?

   a. Yes   b. No

5. Do you suffer from frequent cold or headaches?

   a. Yes   b. No

*If your answers are 1.a, 2.a, 3.a, 4.b and 5.b, then you show signs of being a determined person.

Tips to Parents and Teachers

Experts say that stress is contagious. Your stress can easily get passed on to the children around you. Therefore, it is imperative that as adults, you need to first be in a position to handle any stressful situation of your own. Learn to leave stress behind in your workplace before stepping into your home. At school, create a stress-free ambience where the child and its education is the focal point of all activity. An organized life is generally stress-free.

Encourage a routine in children. Insist on regular sleep timings. Ensure that it is not 'all work and no play' for the child. Physical exercise, playtime and study time have to be balanced in their schedule.

Stress is generally felt when targets are not met or when mistakes are made. Targets can be met when they are set realistically and when schedules are adhered to. As for mistakes, everyone makes them. Teach children to accept their mistakes and prepare them to have enough grit to rectify their mistakes.

Do's and Don'ts

1. Remember to trust yourself. Be strong and never give in to peer pressure. Learn to say 'No'.

2. Vices are easy to acquire. It takes strength to stay away from them. Show yourself your determination in staying away from things bad for you.

3. Exercise regularly.

4. Have a routine and stick with it.

5. Keep going. Pondering over something without acting on it will never solve your problems. The more you act and the sooner you act, the less stress you are likely to face.

6. Have friends. Value their friendship.

7. Be optimistic. Look at the bright side of things.

Learn to Question

What is questioning?

Questioning is the process of asking something for clarification. It also means the ability to doubt the validity of an existing notion or a new idea because of one's own thought and convictions. This stems from disbelief or a doubt in one's mind. It is important to learn to question because this ability will ensure integrity and maintenance of truth and rationality.

Let us read the following poem by Sam Walter Foss to understand a bit more about the reason to question.

The Calf-Path

One day through the primeval wood

A calf walked home as good calves should;

But made a trail all bent askew,

A crooked trail as all calves do.

Since then three hundred years have fled,

And I infer the calf is dead.

But still he left behind his trail,

And thereby hangs my moral tale.

The trail was taken up next day,

By a lone dog that passed that way;

And then a wise bell-wether sheep

Pursued the trail o'er vale and steep,

And drew the flock behind him, too,

As good bell-wethers always do.

And from that day, o'er hill and glade.

Through those old woods a path was made.

And many men wound in and out,

And dodged, and turned, and bent about,

And uttered words of righteous wrath,

Because 'twas such a crooked path;

But still they followed—do not laugh—

The first migrations of that calf,

And through this winding wood-way stalked

Because he wobbled when he walked.

This forest path became a lane,

that bent and turned and turned again;

This crooked lane became a road,

Where many a poor horse with his load

Toiled on beneath the burning sun,

And traveled some three miles in one.

And thus a century and a half

They trod the footsteps of that calf.

The years passed on in swiftness fleet,

The road became a village street;

And this, before men were aware,

A city's crowded thoroughfare.

And soon the central street was this

Of a renowned metropolis;

And men two centuries and a half,

Trod in the footsteps of that calf.

Each day a hundred thousand rout
Followed the zigzag calf about
And o'er his crooked journey went
The traffic of a continent.
A Hundred thousand men were led,
By one calf near three centuries dead.
They followed still his crooked way,
And lost one hundred years a day;
For thus such reverence is lent,
To well established precedent.

A moral lesson this might teach
Were I ordained and called to preach;
For men are prone to go it blind
Along the calf-paths of the mind,
And work away from sun to sun,
To do what other men have done.
They follow in the beaten track,
And out and in, and forth and back,
And still their devious course pursue,
To keep the path that others do.
They keep the path a sacred groove,
Along which all their lives they move.
But how the wise old wood gods laugh,
Who saw the first primeval calf.
Ah, many things this tale might teach—
But I am not ordained to preach.

— Sam Walter Foss

Comprehension questions

Answer the following questions to check your understanding of the story.

1. When according to the poem did the calf walk through the wood and make a trail?

   _____
   _____
   _____

2. What were the other animals mentioned in the poem that walked on the same trail made by the calf?

   _____
   _____
   _____

3. Why do you think many men 'wound in and out, and dodged, and turned, and bent about, and uttered words of righteous wrath'?

   _____
   _____
   _____

4. Why did many a horse 'travel some three miles in one'?

   _____
   _____
   _____

5. Explain the following lines in the context of the poem:

   'For men are prone to go it blind

   Along the calf-paths of the mind,

   And work away from sun to sun,

   To do what other men have done.'

   _____
   _____
   _____

More about the Value

Human beings are born inquisitive. But somewhere down the line, perhaps with age, most human beings seem to lose the will to ask questions. It is extremely essential to ask questions to get answers and to learn more.

> "All our knowledge results from questions, which is another way of saying that questioning is our most important intellectual tool."
>
> — Neil Postman

Asking questions doesn't always imply asking another person. Though this is also crucial because unless you ask another person the right questions, that person would not know what you need or what you have failed to understand. You will not get the answers to all your doubts.

Another aspect about asking questions is questioning the truth behind things. Existing notions have to be questioned to validate them first hand. Superstitions are crushed aside only when people learn to question their relevance and truth.

Progress is possible only when one learns to question. Therefore, questioning is important for the growth of one's own personality as well as the society.

A VALUE FOR ME

He who asks a question is a fool for five minutes; he who does not ask a question remains a fool forever.

Snippet

Socrates was a Greek philosopher and a great educator. It is said that he often taught his students through questions, thereby forcing them to think and come up with answers themselves.

The kinds of questions that he asked are categorized into six types. Some of the questions he often put to his students were:

- Why do you say that?
- How does this relate to our discussion?
- What does this mean?
- Are you saying … or…?

- What else can we assume?
- What would happen if…?
- Do you agree or disagree with…?
- Why is that happening?
- How do you know this?
- What do you think causes…?
- Are the reasons good enough?
- How can I be sure of what you are saying?
- Why is … necessary?
- Who benefits from this?
- What is the difference between … and …?
- How are … and … similar?
- How could you look at it another way?
- What would happen if…?
- How does … affect …?
- Why is … important?
- What else might I ask?
- Am I making sense? Why not?

These questions are still the most relevant ones to ask for any person trying to understand things around him in order to learn and progress.

> "Judge a man by his questions rather than his answers."
> — Voltaire

Exercises

1. Benjamin Franklin once said, "It is the first responsibility of every citizen to question authority."

   Should you question authority? Debate in class, citing examples to prove your point.

Pick any five proverbs of your choice. Question their relevance and justify your stand. For instance, there is a popular idiom 'Too many cooks spoil the broth.' Do you think this is true because cooking is done best when done with concentration and without interference, or it is not true because many hands help make a task easier and many ideas put together help in making a better dish.

a. _____

b. _____

c. _____

d. _____

e. _____

3. Find five words in the grid that imply 'questioning'.

s	c	e	p	t	i	c	a	l
a	u	d	g	a	n	b	y	r
h	r	k	r	u	q	v	t	u
g	i	b	v	e	u	h	s	y
d	o	u	b	t	i	n	g	b
c	u	r	v	y	s	c	z	J
n	s	n	m	u	i	s	i	C
g	u	r	t	n	t	i	n	G
q	u	i	z	z	i	n	g	o
m	s	b	t	r	v	y	u	F
x	d	f	g	t	e	j	k	l

4. Look around you. You must surely find things which you don't understand. For instance, you may wonder why a window always opens out of a room and not into a room or why a bird is never seen sleeping during the day. Jot down at least six questions to which you don't know the answers or would like more clarification about.

_____
_____
_____
_____
_____
_____
_____
_____
_____
_____

Prepare a list of questions that you would want to ask to any one of the following people, if you get a chance to interview them.

   a. Prime Minister of your country
   b. Famous sports personality
   c. A terrorist

   _____
   _____
   _____
   _____
   _____
   _____
   _____
   _____
   _____
   _____
   _____
   _____

Test yourself

Take the following quiz to know how you feel about asking questions and being in doubt.

1. What do you do when in doubt?
   a. Ask questions to clarify your doubts
   b. Resort to finding out the answer by yourself through books and experimenting

2. When someone asks you a question, how do you react?
   a. Do you answer them or say you 'don't know', accordingly
   b. You don't encourage them asking you questions

3. Do you accept things on faith because your religion says so or because your elders say so?

4. Do you question everything taught to you, not because you want to contradict but because you want to understand?

5. Do you ever think that you know everything and don't need to know more?

If your answers are 1.a or b, 2.a, 3.b, 4.a and 5.c then you are a resourceful person. Else, you may want to work on being more resourceful.

Tips to Parents and Teachers

Never snub a child when he or she asks questions. Answer the questions as truthfully as you can. If you do not know the answer to their questions, encourage them to find out the answers through other sources. You could suggest these sources and you have the time find out the answers along with them. Though you do not need to spoon feed them, a little interest in their interest will give them the motivation and desire to satisfy their curiosity and do better.

It is equally important for children to be able to question any fact before accepting it or rejecting it. Evolving times require evolving theories and new practices. If the child is to contribute to a progressive society, it is essential for him or her to be able to question first without accepting things blindly. Therefore, it is essential that as a parent or a teacher, you are ready with answers or are willing to help the child find convincing answers to their questions and doubts.

Do's and Don'ts

> "Asking the right questions takes as much skill as giving the right answers."
> — Robert Half

1. Never be afraid of asking a question.
2. Try to find answers to your doubts by yourself. When you are unable to, do not hesitate to ask the concerned person or an expert.
3. Think and analyze things that you see around you. Question their validity. Be sure of their truth before accepting them.
4. While asking a question, be clear of what you have already understood and what you wish to understand further.
5. Word your question politely.
6. Don't interrupt a person to ask a question. Ask only after the person has finished speaking.

Human Rights

What are human rights?

Simply put, human rights are rights that belong to every person on the planet. Human rights are apparently to be enjoyed by every human being irrespective of his or her nationality, race, religion or gender.

Human rights are often guaranteed by law and are considered universally applicable. Some of the human rights are the right to life, freedom of expression, equality before law, right to work, right to education, right to development and so on.

Let us read the following extract from gripping speech made by Nelson Mandela on December 10, 1993 in Oslo, Norway, while receiving his Nobel Peace Prize to understand about human rights and the need to uphold them.

I am indeed truly humbled to be standing here today to receive this year's Nobel Peace Prize…

We(fellow Africans who won the Nobel Peace Prize) stand here today as nothing more than a representative of the millions of our people who dared to rise up against a social system whose very essence is war, violence, racism, oppression, repression and the impoverishment of an entire people.

I am also here today as a representative of the millions of people across the globe, the anti-apartheid movement, the governments and organizations that joined with us, not to fight against South Africa as a country or any of its peoples, but to oppose an inhuman system and sue for a speedy end to the apartheid crime against humanity.

These countless human beings, both inside and outside our country, had the nobility of spirit to stand in the path of tyranny and injustice, without seeking selfish gain. They recognized that an injury to one is an injury to all and therefore acted together in defence of justice and a common human decency.

Because of their courage and persistence for many years, we can, today, even set the dates when all humanity will join together to celebrate one of the outstanding human victories of our century.

When that moment comes, we shall, together, rejoice in a common victory over racism, apartheid and white minority rule.

That triumph will finally bring to a close a history of five hundred years of African colonization that began with the establishment of the Portuguese empire.

Thus, it will mark a great step forward in history and also serve as a common pledge of the peoples of the world to fight racism wherever it occurs and whatever guise it assumes.

At the southern tip of the continent of Africa, a rich reward is in the making, an invaluable gift is in the preparation, for those who suffered in the name of all humanity when they sacrificed everything – for liberty, peace, human dignity and human fulfillment.

This reward will not be measured in money. Nor can it be reckoned in the collective price of the rare metals and precious stones that rest in the bowels of the African soil we tread in the footsteps of our ancestors. It will and must be measured by the happiness and welfare of the children, at once the most vulnerable citizens in any society and the greatest of our treasures.

The children must, at last, play in the open veld, no longer tortured by the pangs of hunger or ravaged by disease or threatened with the scourge of ignorance, molestation and abuse, and no longer required to engage in deeds whose gravity exceeds the demands of their tender years.

In front of this distinguished audience, we commit the new South Africa to the relentless pursuit of the purposes defined in the World Declaration on the Survival, Protection and Development of Children.

The reward of which we have spoken will and must also be measured by the happiness and welfare of the mothers and fathers of these children, who must walk the earth without fear of being robbed, killed for political or material profit, or spat upon because they are beggars.

They too must be relieved of the heavy burden of despair which they carry in their hearts, born of hunger, homelessness and unemployment.

The value of that gift to all who have suffered will and must be measured by the happiness and welfare of all the people of our country, who will have torn down the inhuman walls that divide them.

These great masses will have turned their backs on the grave insult to human dignity which described some as masters and others as servants, and transformed each into a predator whose survival depended on the destruction of the other.

The value of our shared reward will and must be measured by the joyful peace which will triumph, because the common humanity that bonds both black and white into one human race, will have said to each one of us that we shall all live like the children of paradise.

Thus shall we live, because we will have created a society which recognizes that all people are born equal, with each entitled in equal measure to life, liberty, prosperity, human rights and good governance.

Such a society should never allow again that there should be prisoners of conscience or that any person's human rights should be violated.

Neither should it ever happen that once more the avenues to peaceful change are blocked by usurpers who seek to take power away from the people, in pursuit of their own, ignoble purposes.

In relation to these matters, we appeal to those who govern Burma that they release our fellow Nobel Peace Prize laureate, Aung San Suu Kyi, and engage her and those she represents in serious dialogue, for the benefit of all the people of Burma.

We pray that those who have the power to do so will, without further delay, permit that she uses her talents and energies for the greater good of the people of her country and humanity as a whole.

Far from the rough and tumble of the politics of our own country, I would like to take this opportunity to join the Norwegian Nobel Committee and pay tribute to my joint laureate, Mr. F.W. de Klerk.

He had the courage to admit that a terrible wrong had been done to our country and people through the imposition of the system of apartheid.

He had the foresight to understand and accept that all the people of South Africa must, through negotiations and as equal participants in the process, together determine what they want to make of their future.

But there are still some within our country who wrongly believe they can make a contribution to the cause of justice and peace by clinging to the shibboleths that have been proved to spell nothing but disaster.

It remains our hope that these, too, will be blessed with sufficient reason to realize that history will not be denied and that the new society cannot be created by reproducing the repugnant past, however refined or enticingly repackaged.

We live with the hope that as she battles to remake herself, South Africa will be like a microcosm of the new world that is striving to be born.

This must be a world of democracy and respect for human rights, a world freed from the horrors of poverty, hunger, deprivation and ignorance, relieved of the threat and the scourge of civil wars and external aggression and unburdened of the great tragedy of millions forced to become refugees.

The processes in which South Africa and Southern Africa as a whole are engaged beckon and urge us all that we take this tide at the flood and make of this region a living example of what all people of conscience would like the world to be.

We do not believe that this Nobel Peace Prize is intended as a commendation for matters that have happened and passed. We hear the voices which say that it is an appeal from all those, throughout the universe, who sought an end to the system of apartheid.

We understand their call, that we devote what remains of our lives to the use of our country's unique and painful experience to demonstrate, in practice, that the normal condition for human existence is democracy, justice, peace, non-racism, non-sexism, prosperity for everybody, a healthy environment and equality and solidarity among the peoples.

Moved by that appeal and inspired by the eminence you have thrust upon us, we undertake that we too will do what we can to contribute to the renewal of our world so that none should, in future, be described as the wretched of the earth. Let it never be said by future generations that indifference, cynicism or selfishness made us fail to live up to the ideals of humanism which the Nobel Peace Prize encapsulates.

Let the strivings of us all, prove Martin Luther King Jr to have been correct, when he said that humanity can no longer be tragically bound to the starless midnight of racism and war.

Let the efforts of us all, prove that he was not a mere dreamer when he spoke of the beauty of genuine brotherhood and peace being more precious than diamonds or silver or gold.

Let a new age dawn!

Thank you.

Comprehension questions

Answer the following questions to check your understanding of the story.

1. What social system is Nelson Mandela referring to when he says its very essence is 'war, violence, racism, oppression, repression and the impoverishment of an entire people'?

   _____
   _____
   _____

2. 'Because of their courage and persistence for many years, we can, today, even set the dates when all humanity will join together to celebrate one of the outstanding human victories of our century.'

   Who is the 'their' that Nelson Mandela is referring to in the above lines?

   _____
   _____
   _____

3. How will the reward that South Africa will enjoy be measured in?

   _____
   _____
   _____

4. Mention some of the human rights violations mentioned in the speech.

   _____
   _____
   _____

5. Mention some of the human rights that Mandela wishes for every person to enjoy.

   _____
   _____
   _____

More about the Value

Throughout history, human beings have suffered great atrocities put upon them by other human beings. Be it during times of war, or during times of relative peace where economic gain or social one-upmanship over the other was a priority, people have subjected other fellow human beings to untellable misery and suffering.

It was after the World War II, a time when the world had witnessed one of its largest ever genocide and life loss in war, that the United Nations Universal Declaration of Human Rights (UNDHR) was signed in 1948. It was an attempt by several nations to rebuild a world that would uphold freedom, justice and peace for all.

> To deny people their human rights is to challenge their very humanity.
> — Nelson Mandela

The human rights outlined in the UNDHR are rights held by all people equally and forever.

The human rights are inalienable. These rights cannot be cast aside or lost under any circumstance.

The human rights are indivisible. Every human being is entitled to enjoy every right declared in the UNDHR. No one right can be dismissed because it is apparently less important or not necessary.

The human rights are interdependent. All the rights given to human beings are interdependent. Denying one right will impact the other rights of the human being.

The human rights are equal and non-discriminatory. Every human being, irrespective of his or her race, nationality, religion, culture or gender is granted equal rights.

These rights are both rights and obligatory. This means that while every person is entitled to the rights, it is the State's obligation to ensure that the people enjoy these rights and are not denied these rights under any circumstance.

> The International Human Rights Day is celebrated on December 10th every year.

A VALUE FOR ME

Give to every human being every right you claim for yourself.

Snippet

An estimated 150 million children worldwide are engaged in child labour

Children around the world are routinely engaged in paid and unpaid forms of work that are not harmful to them. However, they are classified as child labourers when they are either too young to work or are involved in hazardous activities that may compromise their physical, mental, social or educational development. The prevalence of child labour is highest in sub-Saharan Africa. In the least developed countries, nearly one in four children (ages 5 to 14) are engaged in labour that is considered detrimental to their health and development.

Around 13 per cent of children aged 5 to 14 in developing countries are involved in child labour. Sub-Saharan Africa has the largest proportion of child labourers (25 per cent of children aged 5 to 14 years). In South Asia, 12 per cent of children in this age group are performing potentially harmful work compared to 5 per cent of children in Central and Eastern Europe and the Commonwealth of Independent States (CEE/CIS), the region with the lowest rate of child labour.

"We will not enjoy security without development,
We will not enjoy development without security,
And we will not enjoy either without respect for human rights."

— Kofi Annan (UN Security General)

Exercises

1. Write a poem or story about human rights. You could also make a video about the need for upholding human rights.

2. Create a collage to show the theme of 'same yet different' to help others understand the need for upholding human rights. You could gather pictures from various sources like newspapers, magazines and the internet.

3. Group activity: On a large chart paper, draw a tree. On its leaves, write various rights that you consider are essential for human beings to live with dignity. Display this chart in your school corridors for all to see and learn.

4. Write a 500 word essay on the following:

> If we can conquer space, we can conquer childhood hunger.
>
> — Buzz Aldrin

5. **Suggested reading to know more about human rights:**
   a. The Diary of a Young Girl by Anne Frank
   b. Hunger Games series by Suzanne Collins
   c. Horton Hears a Who by Dr Seuss

Test yourself

Take the following quiz to check your knowledge on Human Rights.

1. Which one of the following is absolutely prohibited under International Law?
   a. Slavery   b. Death Penalty

2. Complete the following sentence: All human beings are born free and _____ in dignity and rights. (healthy / equal)

3. The number of rights declared in the Universal Declaration of Human Rights is _____. (10 / 30)

4. Which among the following are considered Human Rights Activists?
   a. Gandhiji   b. Martin Luther King   c. Nelson Mandela   d. All three

5. Is child labour considered a violation of human rights?
   a. Yes   b. No

Tips to Parents and Teachers

Accept plurality. Teach children tolerance and the ability to accept the plurality in the world. Bring the practice of upholding human rights closer home.

Ensure that you and your family do not violate basic human rights of others. Ensure that you do not encourage child labour. Ensure that you provide proper pay to your help and other employees. Ensure that you show them empathy, compassion and the respect they deserve.

Point out to children incidents of human rights violation that you may come across in the news. Debate the issue and encourage children to express their views on the violation of human rights and the need to uphold human rights.

Do's and Don'ts

1. Remember that every person is born equal. Never treat someone as inferior.
2. Slavery is banned. No human being should be treated as a slave.

3. Treat every person the way you would want to be treated.
4. Be polite while talking to others.
5. Offer help if you are in a position to.
6. Do not encourage child labour.
7. Don't hesitate to raise your voice against any human rights violation.

> Give to every human being every right you claim for yourself.
> — Robert Ingersoil

My Paragons

Who inspires you to be a better person and a better citizen? Identify your role models. Paste their pictures or sketch their portraits. Write what qualities you like in them and how you would want to fashion yourself around them.